ENCHANTED WONDERS

Nicole Dobrich

authorHOUSE®

AuthorHouse™
1663 Liberty Drive
Bloomington, IN 47403
www.authorhouse.com
Phone: 1 (800) 839-8640

Published by AuthorHouse 06/26/2020

ISBN: 978-1-7283-6526-8 (sc)
ISBN: 978-1-7283-6525-1 (e)

Library of Congress Control Number: 2020911457

Print information available on the last page.

I want to thank my amazing husband, son, parents, and family for believing in me to help bring my dream to life! But most of all I dedicate this book to my son, nieces, and nephews who I want to know that if you put your mind to it you can accomplish anything. A big thank you to Sharon Tan for coloring the underground gnome home featured on the front of my coloring book.

Thank you for purchasing Enchanted Wonders with 37 unique and original coloring pages and 14 additional pages of bookmarks for releasing your creativity. Each image is printed on single sided paper, except for the four double spread coloring pages. Single sided images are great for using different mediums to color with. These pages were created with love and I hope you enjoy it!

Enchanted Wonders is packed full of tiny gnome homes, unicorns, fairies, animals, butterflies, mermaids, ocean life, wizard, witches, and holiday coloring pages. Please make sure you join our Facebook group so you can post your beautiful work in progress and completed coloring pages. The group is called Nicole Dobrich Coloring Book Group. Thank you so much and happy coloring!

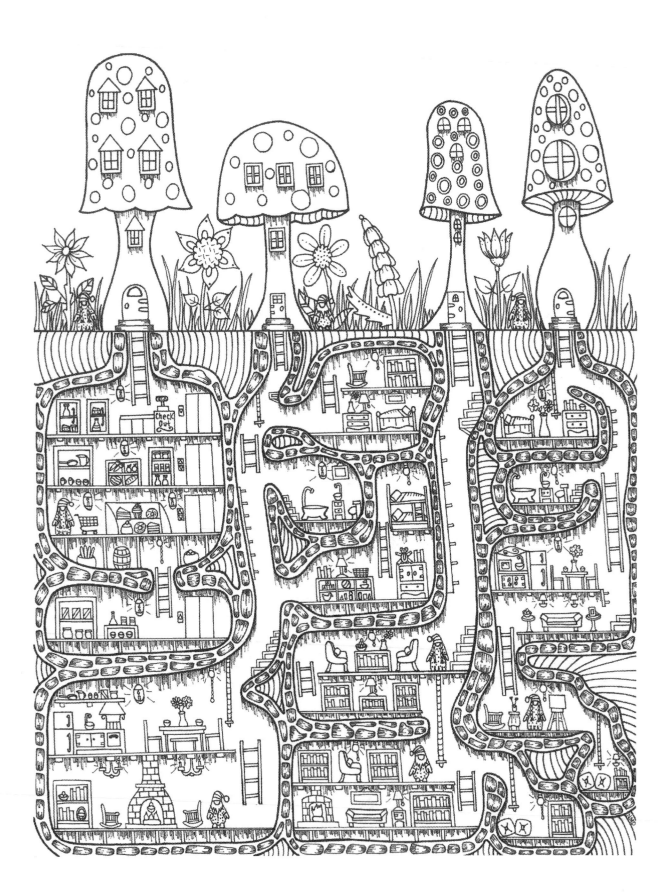

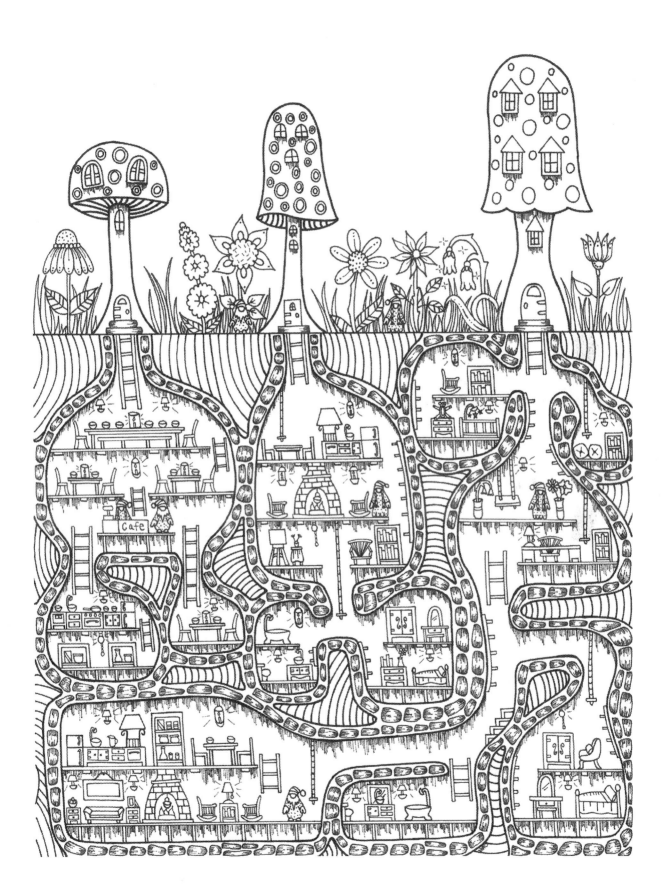

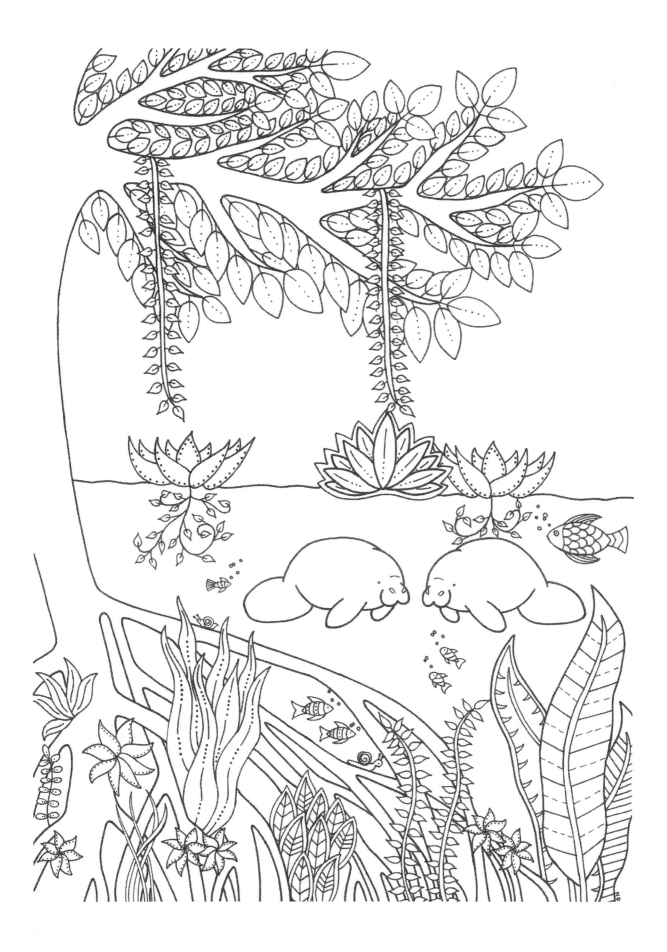

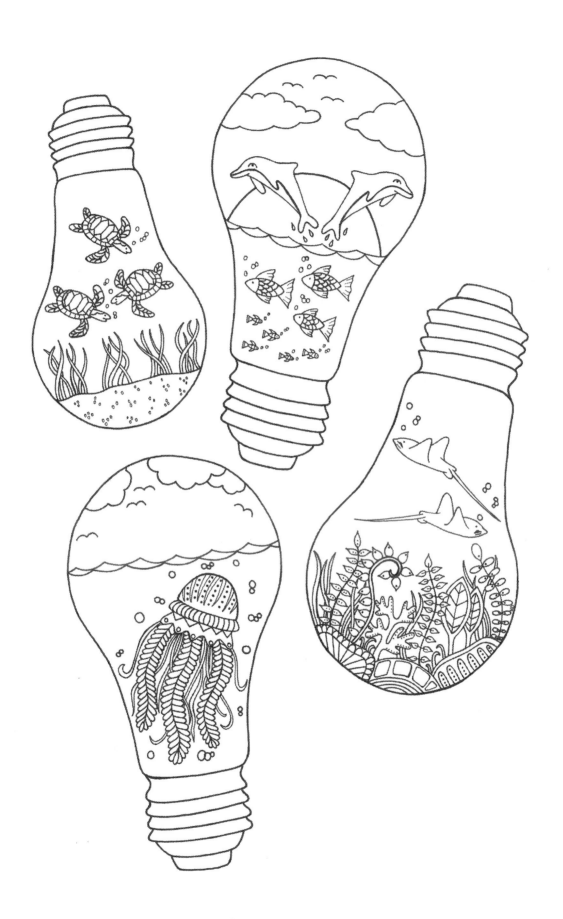

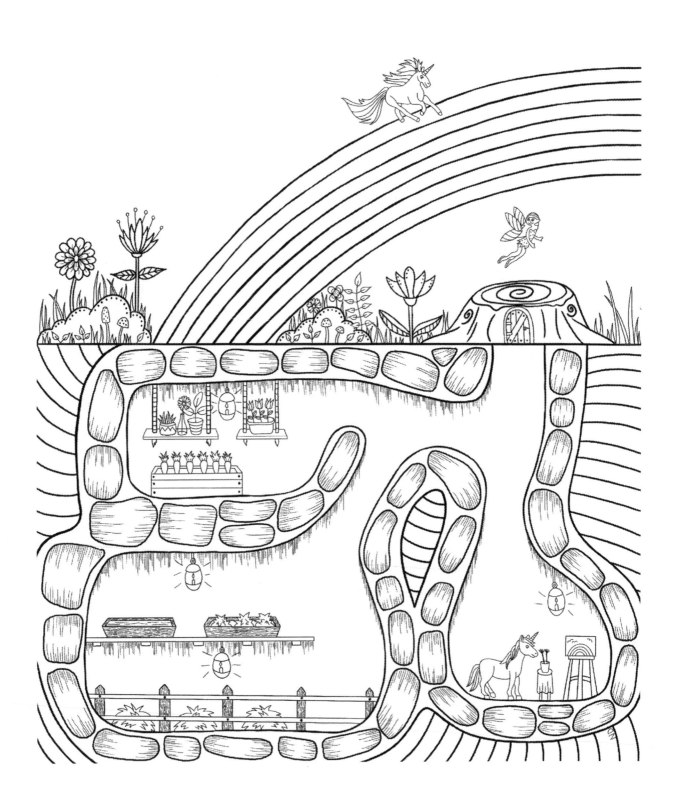

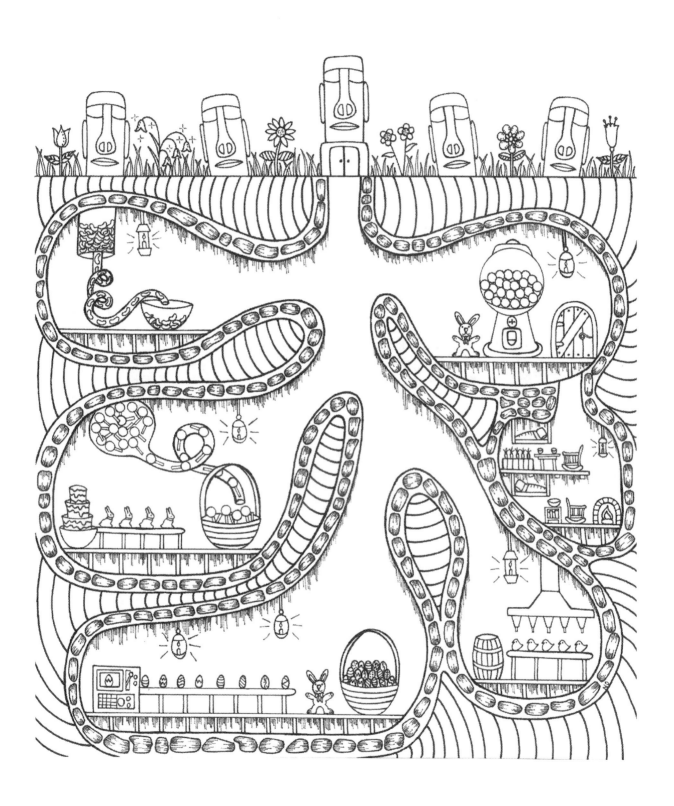

1) Color the front of the RVs
2) Cut out the RVs
3) On the RV page cut the
dotted lines vertically
4) Insert the flap into the
opening and glue it

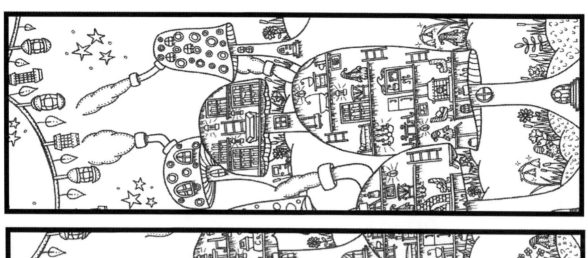

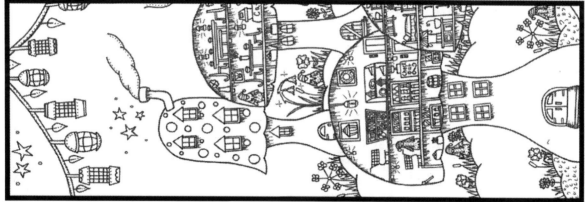

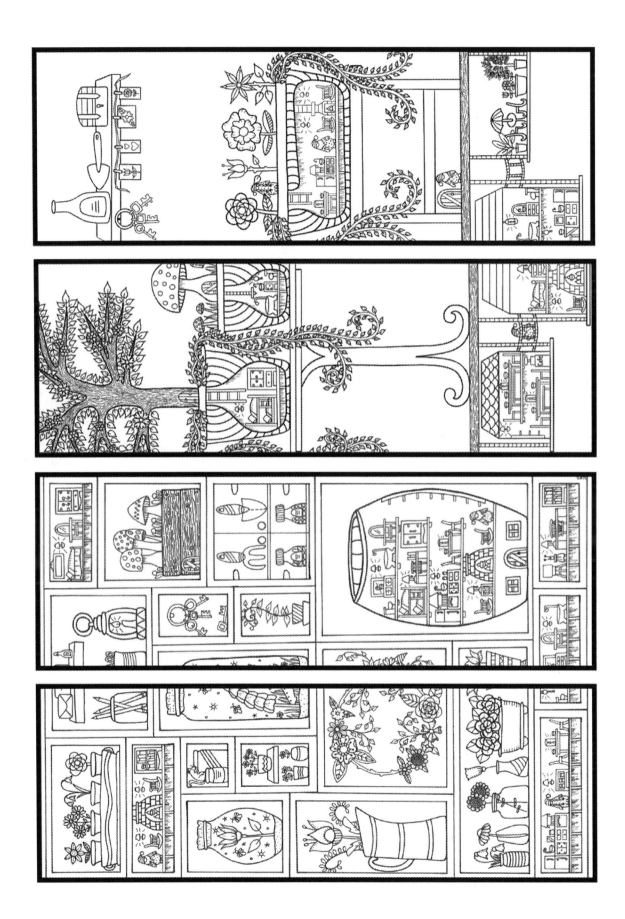

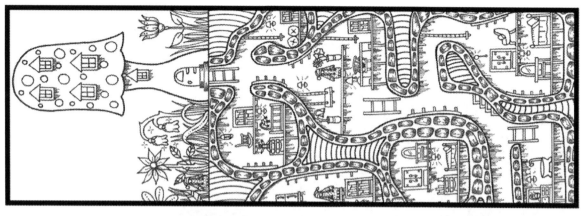

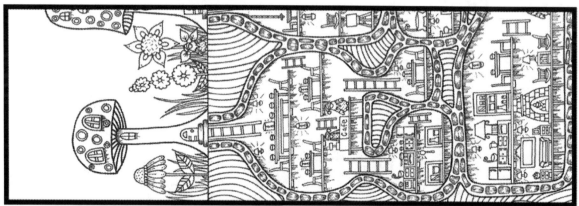

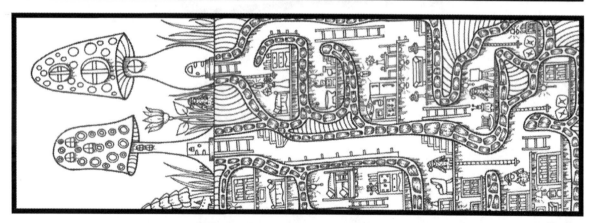

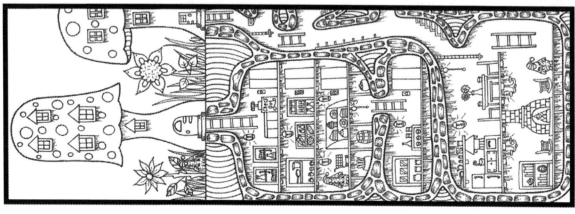

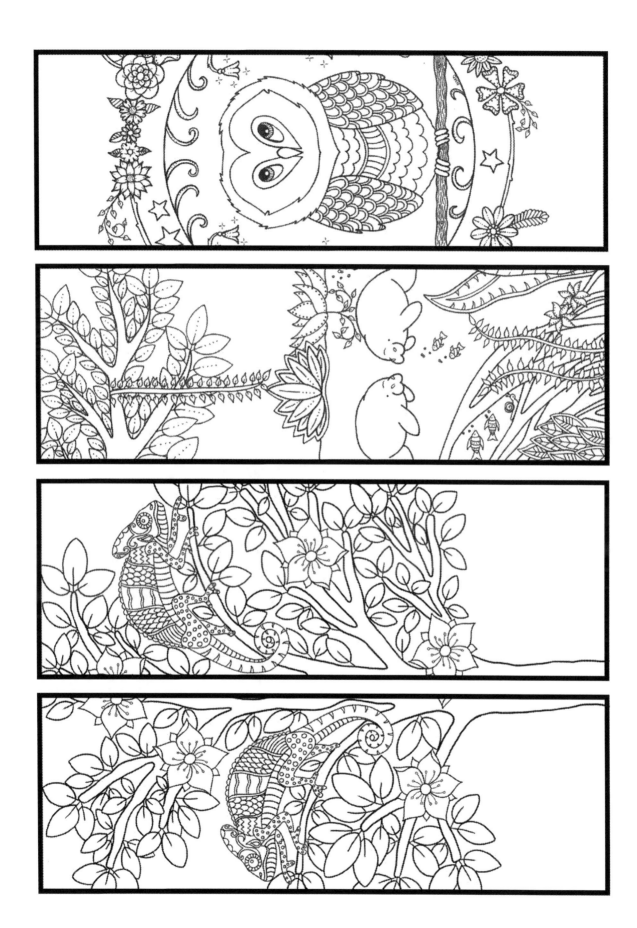

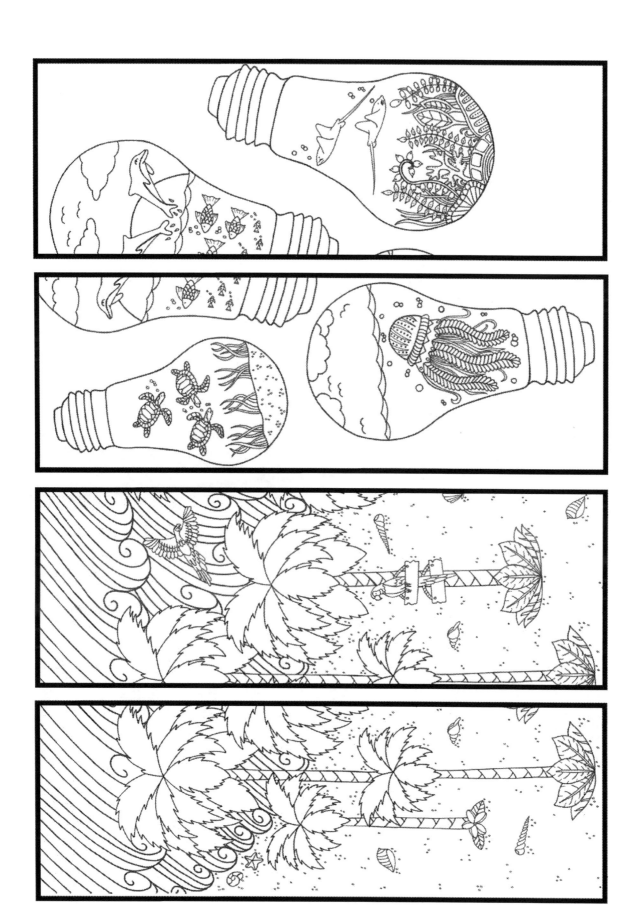

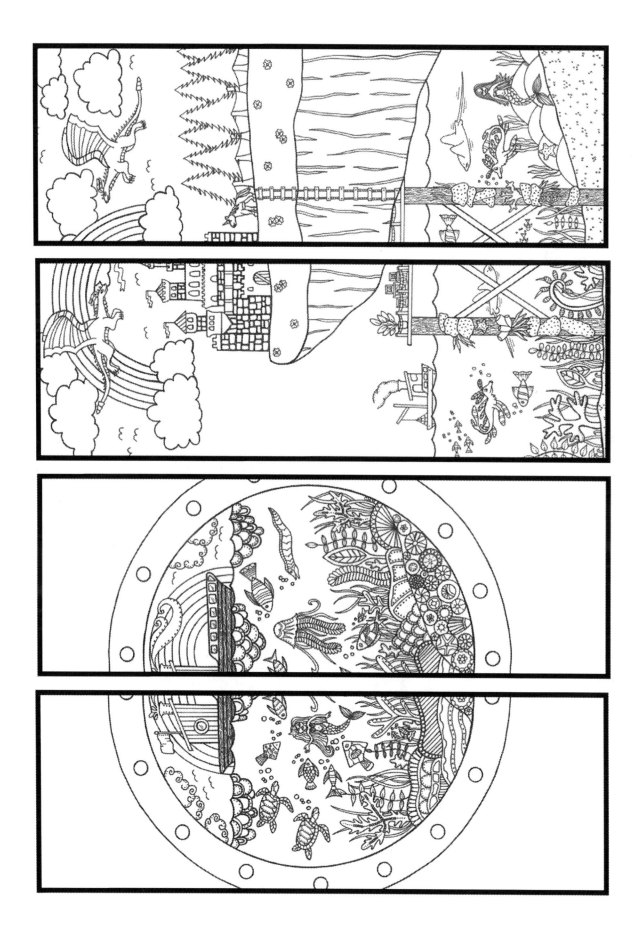

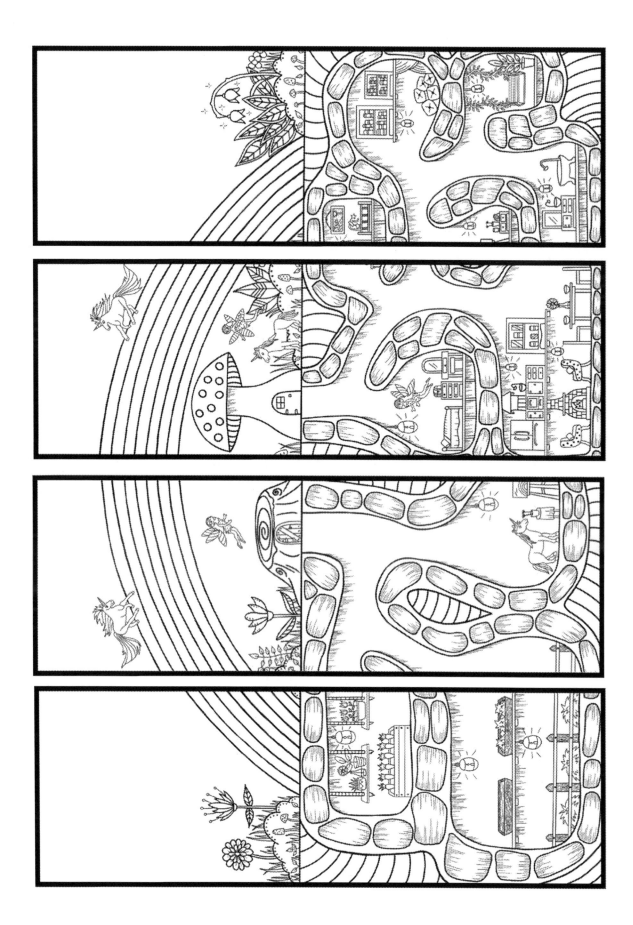

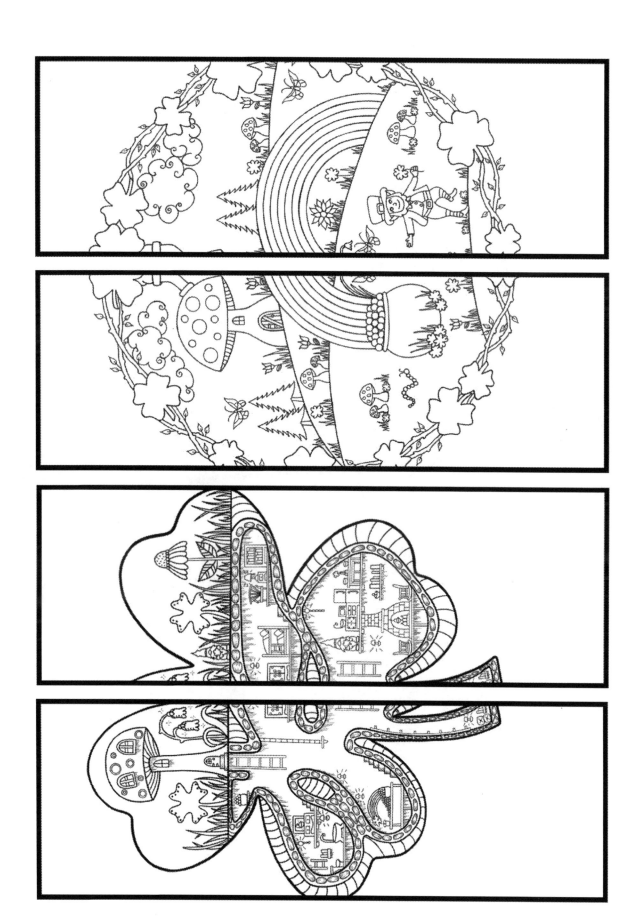

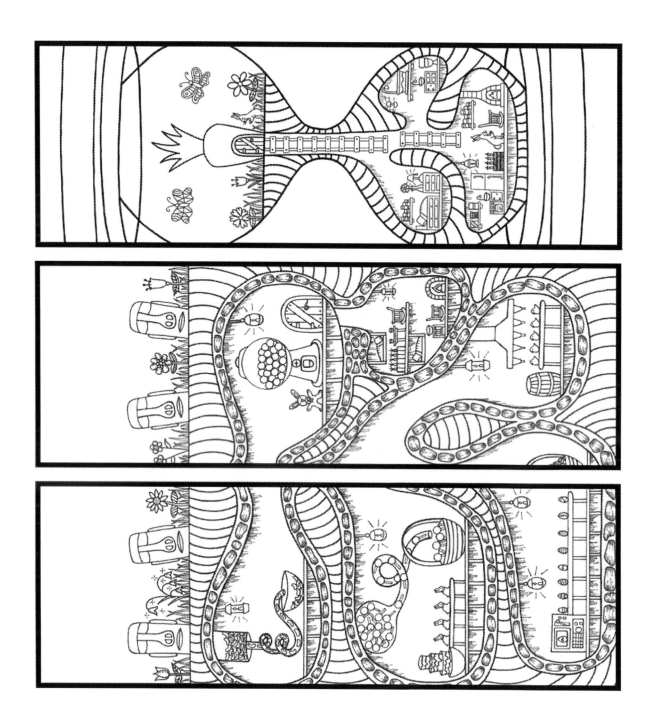

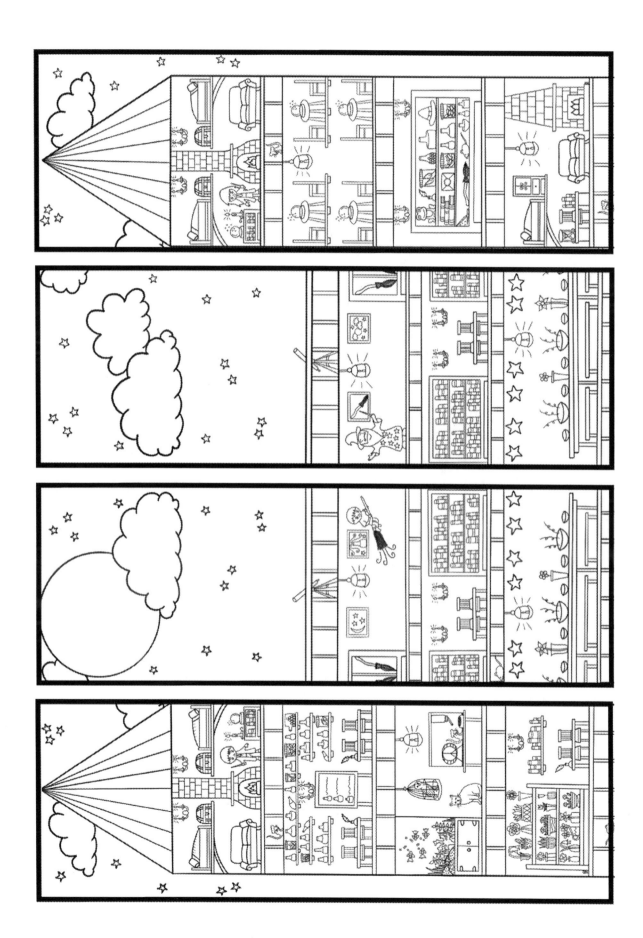

Nicole's 6 year old son Tyler's Drawing

Printed in the United States
By Bookmasters